# THE FETISH PARTY:

## AN UNDERWORLD OF ENERGY, EXCITEMENT, PLEASURE & PAIN

by

PVC Leatherman

# **Table of Contents**

# Foreword

When I got into the "scene" in the mid-Seventies, there was no internet, chat rooms, or FetLife. There were no dungeons, no parties, and no conventions. The hub of activities was the local adult book store. There you could occasionally find contact magazines. Or in the corner, a small bulletin board with business cards tacked to them. If you were lucky enough to have a Pro Mistress practicing in your area, this was how you would find out. The adult book stores themselves functioned at the margins of the law. During election season, police would be motivated to raid massage parlors and book stores to make the incumbent mayor look tough on crime.

With the contact magazines, you often had to mail money and your contact info to the magazine. They would then, hopefully, forward it to the advertiser. Often you did not receive any return contact info. You couldn't blame the magazine, however. Pro Mistresses often had short careers, victims of police "tough on crime" actions too.

With the business cards you could make direct contact with Pro Mistresses in your area, but this was tricky too. They were always on their guard for undercover cops and it took a while to earn their trust. Many operated out of their homes, the idea of a stand alone dungeon did not really start until the Eighties.

Things began to change by the early Nineties. The early internet would feature chat rooms and advertisements. And in Ft. Lauderdale, the Fetish Factory opened its doors. Before this, you could find adult "toys" at book stores or lingerie shops but fetish gear had to ordered through the mail. Finally, here was a local store front where you could find ball gags, manacles, blindfolds, and check the quality of the merchandise before you purchased. You didn't have to buy a "pig in a poke". More importantly, Fetish Factory carried fetish clothing, latex and leather. You could make sure of the size and fit and compare items before you bought.

But now that people could dress up, where could they go? Many of the growing fetish community wanted to do more than just play in their own bedrooms. They wanted to show off, strut their stuff in their new clothes, and they wanted to commune with others who shared their kinks. In 1995, Glenn and Donna, owners of the Fetish Factory came up with the idea of hosting a regular party where only true kinksters could attend, share, and play. To ensure that only community members were allowed in, a strict dress code was enforced. You had to wear latex or leather, no jeans or casual wear. This limited the curious and "tourists" who might otherwise crowd the event.

The first parties were held at clubs very near the Fetish Factory, particularly a place called The Vortex. Entering the dark club with its pulsing music, your first sight was of a fat, naked man being flagellated by a woman in a leather dress and masks You felt as if you were entering the Stygian depths. You were entering a whole, new world. What was most unusual was watching public play. Before this, people would play in their own homes. The more daring would have friends over. But now your flogging your partner would be witnessed by complete strangers. And it was OK. We were all there to share our kinks.

Rules had to be enforced, because some newbies didn't realize that they weren't invited to participate in the scenes they were watching. And certain sexual acts were not allowed-no genital exposure or penetrating acts. The clubs would face loss of their liquor license or being shut down completely if guests were too enthusiastic. But it was all very new back then and the frisson was exciting. Few participants had been able to show off or watch others play, and now it was "out there" for just a modest entrance fee. I recall one young man dressed only in latex shorts being suspended from the ceiling in a hogtie position. Women took turns spinning him around and attempted to land their crops on his crotch as he whirled around.

The parties helped solidified the fetish community, giving members a monthly chance to meet and beat friends, to share and show off, to drink and to dance. New friends were made who shared a secret passion, and new play partners were connected with in a safe environment. Eventually, new dungeons would open and other fetish parties would form. But those first few years were magical and memorable.

- Randy LaBido

# Introduction

Latex, leather, vinyl, whips, paddles, floggers, violet wands, hot candle wax, St. Andrews crosses, stocks, cages, restraints, chastity devices, hot candle wax. Gags, blindfolds, masks, collars, leashes, straitjackets, nipple clamps, clothespins, diapers, sex toys, strap-ons. Foot worship, boot worship, ass worship, whipping, flogging, paddling, spanking, tease and denial. Age play, animal play, pony play, fire play, ice play, impact play, edge play, human furniture, domination, submission, humiliation. Is that enough for you, or do you desire more? How about much, much more? Those are minute samples in the underworld of kink and fetish you will see and possibly experience at fetish parties. This book is to serve as your introduction to fetish parties- events that allow people to observe and indulge in taboo activities that the majority of people do not understand, find gross, or consider utterly perverse. It is an intense environment-one which can be fascinating, enlightening, and extremely pleasurable, but by all means, not scary. Let's begin!

# I

# What Fetish Parties Are and Are Not

Recently, I invited three groups of vanilla [defined in Chapter II] friends to a free fetish party. This particular party was a customer appreciation party with no cover [usually there is a standard cover for men and women], free parking, and 2-4-1 drinks from 10pm-11pm. Their age ranges were late 20's to mid 40's. The first was a handsome young fellow in his late 20's, who was a natural with women. He was afraid he would catch a STD (sexually transmitted disease) because he thought I was inviting him to an orgy! I had invited him to a gangbang prior to that. Apparently, that was where his mind remained. I text him pictures of party goers, BDSM (Bondage Discipline Dominant & Submissive, Sadism and Masochism), and other play scenes [fetish activity involving two or more people]. No matter how much I assured him nothing would threaten his health or life, he declined. He told me a girl he dated was interested, but not him. Next, was a hulking fellow in his late 30's to early 40's. I told him he should come with his wife so they both could share the experience. He was all for going--no questions asked. But when his wife saw how the women were dressed, she decided neither of them would be going! The third was a fun-loving woman in her mid 40's who saw me a few times in my fetish attire en route to a party. She turned beet red when I invited her! Later, I sent her pictures, and received a frogs and crickets response.

Everyone had preconceived notions about what fetish parties were. No amount of explaining would make them budge! I told them they could simply look, and if it was too much for them, they could leave. However, if they enjoyed what they saw, they would know what to expect at future parties, ones with cover charges.

After those unexpected turn downs, I truly need to explain here what fetish parties are, and aren't. Otherwise, you too may continue to think as they had. This should eliminate any misconceptions you may have about the parties and their guests.

The first time I became aware of such things was merely two years ago in May 2014 at a high-rise hotel. And I do not mean a run-of-the-mill one. I'm talking one with suites, a huge pool, and a top notch indoor restaurant. I was meeting a well-known International fetish model and DJ for a foot fetish shoot. She also hosted huge fetish parties in Canada. Once inside the hotel, I marveled at what I saw. I felt as if I was Luke when he stepped foot inside Chalmun's Cantina in Star Wars! It was the Fetish Factory 19th Annual Anniversary Fetish Weekend: four days, nine parties, which includes after parties.

Fetish Factory was the originator of the glam fetish scene in North America. I obtained some very specific details from the Glenn, owner of FF and host to Alter Ego, XFP, and the Fetish Weekend events:

1) FF pioneered the fetish community in Florida.

2) FF was the first to create Fetish Glam fetish parties in North America back in 1995.

3) FF hosts ONLY strict dress code fetish parties while all the rest copy or emulate our events.

4) FF is the only event in the USA that not only has a strict dress code it is the only event that STICKS by their dress code.

5) Other events charge more if you are no in dress code while FF refuses to destroy the integrity of the event and refuses admission.

6) FF refuses to allow open photography for the privacy of the crowd other events allow mobile phone photography.

7) FF hosts the largest and most talked about international Fetish Weekend and one of the only organizers to but out huge hotels for their fetish weekend which attracts people from over 35 countries.

...because without FF there would never be such a party and if you travel you will see just how different our events compare to any other event in the US and the world!

People from numerous countries came to attend. The event draws the most well-known fetish models from all over the world, many of whom are headliner performers at the four parties. They are also the ones who usually have the most over-the-top outfits! Much of the hotel staff was probably in the same state of shock I was, although they had been prepped for the event. Men and women were scantily dressed in latex shorts and bikinis, ready-to-wear and custom. Others were decked out in ready-to-wear and custom leather outfits, and vinyl wear. Both sexes led each other by leashes, or wear shrouded by masks or hoods. I went to the dungeon, and befriended the dungeon mistress and a female guest who hosted fetish parties in North Carolina. They asked if I was going to any of the parties, and I told them I wasn't. Of course, they pressed me for a reason--mine was attire. Eager for me to experience their underworld, they quickly gave me a crash course on how to dress for a fetish party, and told me where to buy the attire. Yes, you guessed it. Fetish Factory!

Next day, I was half-and-half. I had a black, PVC vinyl military shirt, white dress pants, and black dress shoes. They applauded me on my first piece of fetish wear, but I still needed more. I told a friend about it, and directed me to an online store which specialized in leather wear for motorcyclists. There came a July 4th special, which was right up my alley. I bought my first pair of leather pants from it. They were a size too big because I read reviews which said to buy them a size larger then regular. After using some hemming glue, they were ready. I hit an Army-Navy surplus store, and bought a pair of combat boots with the store's online coupon. Yes, I'm a thrifty spender! While there, I also bought a pair of handcuffs. They were my second pair. The first, I bought in the toy section of a retail store. Believe it, or not, they looked better than the Army-Navy ones, and were just as functional! Finally, I bought a leather cap online, which convert from a derby cap to a military style hat. It was finally time to go to my first party!

Fetish parties are nothing more than kinky costume parties. As one of my friends put it, "It's like a vanilla party, but with different attire." There will be a plethora of people from all walks of life, dressed in various styles of fetish fashion. I stress the word "fashion" because it is one big show. People constantly compliment each other on what they are wearing. Some buy their outfits, custom order them, or make them by hand. You will see people dancing to EDM (Electronic Dance Music) from a variety of DJs, or recent music from local bands, having drinks [alcohol and non alcohol], socializing, making out, in play scenes, or getting sexual. If you pay close attention, you will notice those same things take place at regular nightclubs between people dressed in everyday clothes.

If you were to dress people at regular nightclubs in fetish wear, they would become much less inhibited, guaranteed. Think of all the sexy shenanigans taking place during Halloween. It is the one night where people can dress up and cut loose. And when you add dancing, drinking, and club hopping to the equation, well.... Not be crass, but Halloween is the main holiday night women are most likely to hook up with random guys. It is also the one night a guy can dress in a costume which fully covers him, and still get laid-even more than New Years Eve! Being in costume is a powerful aphrodisiac! The same for fetish attire. We will get more into that later. But for now, I just want you to know the basics of fetish parties.

They are not Caligula style orgies hosted by a degenerate ruler.[2] They are not sex clubs, sex-fetish clubs, swingers clubs, or strict BDSM clubs.[4] Just so you know, you are not guaranteed sex at a sex club. Imagine paying a big entry fee, or annual membership fee, and nobody wants to swing or have sex with you. That would be brutal. Or imagine you not finding anyone who you want to swing or have sex with there. One young guest came to a party ready for some action. Oh man, was his motor revving! I told him what the party was, and definitely what it wasn't. He ended up walking around the venue like a lynx hungry for a rodent! After a while, he called it a night, and left.

If you come by yourself, most of the same rules apply as if you were going to a regular nightclub. Don't be rude, don't be a bitch, jerk, or asshole, be social and have fun. Simple.

Fetish parties are truly unique environments where like-minded people go to enjoy themselves, drink, dance, socialize, and watch or take part in activities, which mainstream society deems taboo, freaky, or kinky. I recommend you watch the online documentary, "I am Fetish" by Kyle Farley for a visual aid.

# II

# Vanillas and Fetishists

It has been two years in, and I'm not "hardcore" fetishist. I am a basic fetishist, and have been since age four. But as with many fetishists, we keep our fetishes hidden for fear of humiliation, ridicule, degradation, blacklisting, abuse, or violence. According to the YouTube documentary "I am Fetish" by Kyle Farley, the world view on fetishism hasn't changed over the past 400 years. European in origin, "feitico" was Portuguese for "false power". It was a term used to ridicule Africans who worshiped idols. Fast forward to modern times, "The World Health Organization (WHO) classifies fetish behavior as a mental illness."[1]

During my first visit to the anniversary weekend dungeon, I saw a man built like a power lifter, baseball player, or football wide receiver...wearing a corset, high-heeled platform boots, restrained to a St. Andrews cross [defined in Chapter IX], and flogged by a woman. This year, I saw a guy with a similar build, walked around wearing a diaper. Later, I found out he was a high-powered attorney. I saw women with strap-ons focusing their attention on women and men alike. Women dressed as little girls, and wore their hair in kind. Guys wore school uniforms with backpacks. Women got their shoes and feet kissed, rubbed, licked, and worshiped. Someone was tied to a table, and had hot candle wax dripped on them. Maybe someone was bound with rope to the point they could not move. They are fetishists. People who engage in the things that turn them and others on the most. No judgements. Sometimes it is purely experimental. I have been flogged, whipped, knifed, and violet wanded. Neither of those did it for me. I received a tutorial on how to flog someone, which I enjoyed. I also took in the explanation of how pain and pleasure works on a physiological and psychological level.

Vanillas are those who aren't into the BDSM or fetish lifestyle. The term can apply to daily usage, e.g. having a vanilla job or vanilla life. Basically, it is those who don't do anything kinky. Sometimes fetishists have to act or be vanilla when it comes to their relationships and sex lives. Imagine the repercussions of a very masculine man, married with children, a pillar in his community, and well-respected, if he were to admit to his wife that he secretly wore her dresses when she was not at home, and bought women's shoes that fit him. Even worse, what if his wife or children caught him doing it! Imagine a woman telling her religious, metro sexual husband, she wants him to brush her hair, then pull it hard, and talk dirty to her. And what about all of the sights I mentioned in the paragraph before this one? That is why we generally keep our fetishes hidden. The ramifications of admitting them, or having them exposed could be significant.

So what is a fetishist to do when in a vanilla relationship, or leading a vanilla life? Drum roll please. Go to a fetish party!

# III

# Finding Them

Do not expect to look inside your local newspaper to find an ad for a fetish party. You may find one in your local New Times, but that is rare. Tickets are sold directly at a store or website owned by a party host, as Fetish Factory does. Or they are sold at designated adult novelty stores affilated with the host, as German Fetish Ball Weekend, Sin City Fetish Night, and Submission South Beach does. Save a few dollars by purchasing your ticket ahead of time instead of at the door. As the title of the book states, a fetish party is an underworld of pleasure and pain. So word of mouth is usually the best way to go to one. How does a fetishist or a vanilla bring up a fetish party in conversation? Timing. If you are talking about parties in general with people, ask if anyone ever heard of fetish parties, and see what they say. Be inquisitive, but not the point you will tip your hat to wanting to attend one. Another much less obvious way is to hit the Internet. That will probably be option number one. One website designed primarily for that is FetLife. Boasting nearly six million members, FetLife is loaded with kinksters, companies who specialize in adult novelty items, and bdsm and fetish events worldwide. A variety of people and companies host fetish parties, thereby making them totally different. Each one is unique to the host and the venue. You may have to travel if you cannot find one in your area. So unless you are in the know, FetLife is definitely the way to go.

# IV

# Preparing Yourself

When in Rome...right? Depending on the host, there can be a strict dress code, or a lax one. Assume the first, unless otherwise stated in the guest attire requirements. You need not break the bank to acquire attire for a fetish party. Latex, can be pricey in store and online, but there are deals. Leather is the middle child, and most well-known attire. PVC or vinyl is the least expensive of the three. It provides the shiny look of latex, the style of leather, and the lowest cost. During my attire tutorial at the dungeon, the women pointed out one guy who had no shirt, but wore a pair of latex or vinyl boxer shorts, black socks, and black sneakers. They told me that was good enough to get him into any fetish party. If his shorts were latex, they were $60, or less. If they were PVC, they could have been half that amount. I invited two vanillas, a boyfriend and girlfriend who weren't in the scene, per se, but knew about fetishes and kink. I scheduled a foot fetish shoot with her the next day. So that night would've been the first time we met. They scrambled from adult video store to adult video store to find him something to wear. Finally, they hit Hustler, and got him a pair of fetish boxer shorts. He came as a boxer, complete with his own hoodie, black socks, and black sneakers.

Women will enjoy the beauty of a gracious double standard, they need not have latex, leather, or vinyl-they simply need to dress sexy! It helps even more when they wear all black, or other dark color. I once saw a beautiful, buxom brunette wearing a tight-fitting blue skirt, and closed-toe, blue wedges. She was without a doubt the most beautiful woman there that particular night. I later ran into her in a play room area, and offered a foot massage for her tired feet. She asked would it just be a massage, and I assured her it would, so she accepted. Oh, how beautiful, her wide, high-arched feet were...and stinky too, just like her sexy shoes! We were joined by a young woman I never met before, but who knew the brunette I met. Next thing I knew, I had four feet to pamper and worship. It was the first time for the one in blue. The other was dressed in all black, had knee-high goth boots, and socks that punched my nose like Manny Pacquiao! She had pretty feet though, so I got over it.

If you do not have access to a local brick-and-mortar establishment which sells sexy or fetish attire, then go online. Be sure to know the store policy on returns. You may also find more than just clothes. Heck, you may want to find more than just clothes! You may want to tie someone up, or be tied. Flog someone, or be flogged. Maybe you want to be led by a leash, handcuffed, or wrapped up in bondage tape.

This is your fetish, or your experimental time with a fetish, so do not hold back.

# V

# Kinky Costume Party

Before you walk inside, you should have a good idea of what to expect in terms of outfits. If you went online to look for fetish clothing for yourself, surely you saw examples of people in full fetish gear. Fetish fashion originated in London, and started with the leather styles so many are familiar with, think back to the Blue Oyster Bar in "Police Academy 1-4". It transitioned to vinyl and latex, and other countries entered the market: Germany, United States, Canada, China, Australia, Netherlands, Pakistan.[4] Just as venue changes keep things fresh for everyone, so do theme changes. There are cyber-based themes, cosplay themes, holiday themes, and any other a party host can creatively imagine. One of the most popular themes is back to school. The Catholic school girl outfit is a classic staple, which never grows old. And since parties are usually thrown once or twice a month, there is a different theme each time. You can have fun just people watching. It is just one big, kinky costume party!

# VI

# Various Venues

Unlike a nightclub, fetish parties tend to move. This looks great for the host, and breaks any tedium for the guests. The same way vanillas enjoy going to various nightclubs and parties to have fun, fetishists feel the same way. You may be surprised to know the very nightclub you were at one night, became the venue for a fetish party the very next! I remember one time when a foot party was held at a dance ballroom after hours. A foot party is where male guests pay an entrance fee, and for $20, they get to mingle with various women, and indulge in their shoe and foot fetishes. The better ones have theme rooms: office, doctor, bubbles, baby oil. Foot fetish is the largest fetish out there, but also one of the least understood thanks to societal norms. Generally, there is no alcohol, but food is served.

Along with the usual crowd, various venues draw new faces. Sometimes distance is the draw for people-closer means convenient. This means an opportunity to meet new fetishers for upcoming parties, or vanilla activities and occasions. Sometimes traveling, national and international fetish models, or music bands who are touring, perform at these venues.

As I previously stated, all the creature comforts of a regular nightclub are in place, along with the same safety measures. Fetish parties have security and bouncers. Someone regularly patrols the designated parking area(s) to ensure no smash and grabs. The key is for the host to select venues which are unique, provide plenty of space for play, private rooms for play, may have upstairs and downstairs, a stage, and multiple bars. One of my personal favorite venues is a strip club. On nights when we share one particular club [it is comprised of two parts, and has an upstairs VIP], I enjoy going over to the dancer side of the club, and offering dancers foot massages. It usually starts with them cringing and protesting when they see me getting ready to sniff their shoes. But after I explain it in a way they understand, they are totally cool with it, and their feet being stinky. Next comes some much enjoyed foot worship, which for many of them is their first experience. T&A (tits & ass) guys usually care less about feet, so they never give girls foot rubs, let alone worship their feet.

The biggest fetish party events draw national and international visitors, and have individual parties at various venues. One imperative venue is the hotel in which guest will stay. Sometimes there is a mass influx of visitors, so there is usually a secondary hotel for the overflow. Fetish Factory always makes sure to have a secondary hotel for its annual Fetish Factory Anniversary Weekend in May. The main hotel has a Pervy Pool Party on Sunday, which many consider as the highlight of the event.

Montréal Fetish Weekend features fashion shows and red carpet events. German Fetish Ball Weekend includes a Breakfast&Farewell. So yeah, venue changes are awesome!

# VII

# The Door

Each fetish party is different based on the host and venue. At one particular venue, which was a nightclub that regularly host big name music artists as well as up and coming artists who either play alone, or open for the more popular artists. Security outside checks all bags, and may prohibit certain props, depending on the kind of prop you have. That is the exception. Usually, you are greeted outside or inside by someone who has flyers for the future parties, or access cards to view the photos and video the event photographers shoot. You will encounter a wide variety of people before you set foot in the venue. This is an excellent time to introduce yourself to people who interest you, or just to be social. People generally enjoy sincere compliments. So use them to get to know others. I made a few really good friends at the door, one was a die hard foot fan. The other two liked feet, but to a lesser degree. Think small, medium, and large in terms of their affinity levels.

As with any social event, it is good to make friends with those who are unable to enjoy themselves by partaking in the fun because they are working. Befriend the person handing out flyers, the one accepting the cover charge, the one handing out the tickets, if applicable. Befriend the coat check person. Everyone is integral to the mechanics of the party. My friends have bought drinks or entertained those who could not leave their post for the night. Good karma comes from being nice to people, and treating them like people instead of workers on the payroll. It goes a long way in their books, as well as the host's because word gets around.

# VIII

# Protocols and Permission

This is the part I explained to everyone who declined to come to the free fetish party. Nothing will happen that you do not want to happen. Single women...no guy is going to come grope you simply because you are scantily dressed in fetish wear. No guy is going to catch you off guard while you are sitting, snatch off your shoe, and start sucking your toes. No guy is going to pick you up, carry you to a table, tie you up, and inundate your body with electricity. Single men...no woman is going to come grope you simply because your package is showing through your fetish boxers. No woman is going to start flogging or spanking you out of the blue. No woman is going to attach a leash to your collar and walk you around the venue, standing or on all fours. Not without permission. There are protocols to follow, and permission which needs to be given. Many fetishists take their D/s (Dominant/submissive) roles seriously. You may want to do some research to understand some social dynamics involved.

If you see a couple, one is holding a leash, the other is at the other end, wearing a collar. Whom do you address? You address the dominant (Dom/D), or dominatrix (Domme/D). The sub (s) may not be allowed to interact or speak without permission. Sometimes both people are wearing collars-then what? They may or may not belong to each other. They may also belong to others. If you are unsure of the dynamic, then address them both, and go from there. You are basically following the same social courtesies and giving the same respect you would at a regular party or nightclub. Just because a man and woman are together doesn't mean they are a couple. One very powerful question to establish unknown relationships is this one: "How do you know each other?" If you know the dynamic, and want to interact or speak with the submissive, then you must ask for permission from the dominant or alpha [male or female]. Some people are there without any restrictions, but do have limits. So if you meet someone, and want to engage in a scene with them, establish the do's, don'ts. This is how to "negotiate" a scene. For example, a woman might say, "You can suck my toes, but don't lick my feet."Or "You can play with my nipples, but don't squeeze my breasts." A man might say, "Just whip me lightly, and just on my back." Or "You can tie me up, but don't cover my head with anything because I want to be able to see." If needed, establish a "safe word". A safe word is an established word that means stop--no more.

This may seem contradictory, but do not be a permission boy or girl. Meaning, do not ask permission for each and every thing. Use good judgement when escalating a scene, the same as with a vanilla interaction. As a man, would you ask a woman if you could hold her hand? As a woman, would you ask a man if you could walk closer to him? Being a permission boy or girl is a huge turn off. Also, while scening, do not solely focus on the fetish or activity itself. Be mindful and engage the person who trusting you and giving you the privilege of playing with them. Otherwise, it can be considered pure objectification, and that person may never play with you again.

What I say next may be painful, but it has to be said. Not

everyone can play or scene with you. Not everyone wants to play or scene with you. People have their reasons: good or bad. Sometimes they will state them, other times they won't. Try not to get "butt hurt about it", as someone on FetLife put it. And definitely don't harass anyone who declines your request. Remain positive, don't take it personally, and continue to have fun. If you do those things, you will find someone even more awesome who will play or scene with you.

Earlier, I mentioned event photographers. They are the ones specifically allowed to shoot photo and video at fetish parties. That is for privacy reasons. So you or your scene may be their focus...with your permission, of course. Think in terms of what happens in Vegas, stays in Vegas. Fetish parties provide guests with access to the stills and video afterward.

Regarding scenes. Do not interrupt scenes you are not invited to join. Give enough room to the players, especially if they are in a scene which may involve impact play, such as flogging, whipping, or caning. Not only might you distract the players, you might be injured in the process from being too close of proximity to the action. Play scenes can be intense and intimate. Submissives sometimes go into a trance-like state called "sub space". It is a point of almost no return, and only the dominant should be the one to bring them back to "vanilla space". Interrupting them is liken to someone interrupting you during sex, while you masturbate, or if you are in the bathroom to jettison some weight, and someone bangs on the door like a crazy person!

# IX

# Instruments of Destruction

I love that song by N.R.G, although it played during a very sad part in "Transformers: The Movie" (1986). Simply dressing in fetish attire is sometimes not enough. If you are in exploratory mode, then you may want to buy a flogger, whip, cane, riding crop, bondage rope, bondage tape, chastity device, violet wand, handcuffs, spreader bar, blindfold, Wartenberg wheel, or any other toy which you fancy giving a spin. Fetish parties will usually have the obligatory St. Andrews cross. I did not explain what that was earlier because I did not want to spoil it. It is a large, wooden or metal "X", which with people are bound facing the cross or with their backs to the cross. There are also leather-bound tables to restrain people, as well as other leather-bound type furniture which resembles a bucking bronco in a country bar. Guests sit on top of them, or bend over them.

If you are inexperienced with any of these instruments, take the time to learn how to use them-for your safety as well as those with who may be on the receiving end of them.

# X

# Get Your Kink On

You should now be ready to walk into a fetish party with confidence! But if not, then you will build up to it. Many experience approach and social anxiety, while others are approach machines and social to the point they approach anyone and everyone. Most people are as nervous about meeting new, so the playing field is level. Make it your mission to speak to and make small talk with at least one person. Next, a couple, and then a group. Remember, there is nothing wrong with people watching. It can be a blast. But if you can become more involved, that is all the better. In fact, that was how I had my first scene at my very first fetish party.

I wore my new gear for the first time. Yes, I fit the bill, but was nervous...still in awe of everything. There was so much going on, so many fascinating people! As I made my way around the club, I noticed a buxom blonde at the bar. She was attractive, wore a latex dress, and black platform sling backs. As she stood at the bar, I saw her give the telltale signal that her feet ached, when she lifted her leg almost 45 degrees, and rotated her foot. I used that observation for my opener. She immediately took me up on my offer for a foot rub, and we walked over to a chair for her to sit. I took off her size 7.5 US shoe and sniffed it. Her shoes were still rather new, so sadly, there was no odor. As I rubbed her high-arched feet, I sniffed them. She enjoyed the attention with no issue. I moved on to kissing her feet. It was when I sucked her toes, that she looked down at me, and told me I had to ask permission. After that, I became her official foot slave at the parties! Little did I know, she was best friends with Donna, and had been going to the parties since day one, nearly 19 years ago! She tried to get Donna to get a foot rub, but she was busy helping run the party. I did not find out until much later found out who they both were. You never know who you may be meeting and scening with, so make sure you are always on your best behavior!

Since that first night, I became very good friends with eight amazing people. We socialize, drink, dance, and play at the parties. We also do vanilla stuff away from the parties. And I met four other friends who share the same unique first name with me. I went on to meet and play with countless numbers of guests, as well as do foot fetish shoots with some of them. These were no small feats because I consider myself an introvert.

You may go to a few parties before you meet anyone, or have a scene. It's ok. We all crawled before we walked, and walked before we ran. Do not let fear be a barrier. You have already taken your first step into a much larger world...and underworld at that! So be a participant instead of merely a spectator. Be open-minded and inquisitive. You may discover you enjoy a fetish you would never have fathomed all thanks to a fetish party!

# Resources

## Clothing

*http://fetish-factory.com*
*http://stores.ebay.com/dark-pleasures-store*
*http://stores.ebay.com/partyboisrubber*
*http://latexcatfish.com*
*http://libidex.com*
*http://latexexpress.com*
*http://twistmyrubberarm.com*
*http://leatherup.com*
*http://leathercult.com*
*http://www.collarfactory.com*
*http://www.thecollarshop.com*

## Equipment

*http://stockroom.com*
*http://extremerestraints.com*
*http://medicaltoys.com*
*http://bdsm-gear.com*
*http://ebay.com*
*http://amazon.com*

## Community

*http://fetlife.com*
*http://thefetishparty.com*

# Fetish Documentaries

[1.] "I am Fetish" (2009)

Kyle Farley

Beyond Vanilla (2001), Claes Lilja

Fetishes (1996), Nick Broomfield

## Fetish Books

Fetish (2007), David Bramwell

Fetish: Fashion, Sex, & Power (1997), Valerie Steele

Fetish News Articles

5 Weird Fetishes That Are More Normal Than You Think (2016)

Laura Tedesco

[2.] http://miami.racked.com/2015/2/13/8030399/fetish-parties

Ashley Brozic

[3.] http://www.berlinlogs.com/2015/05/7-tips-for -going-to-sex-fetish-club-in.html

Lynette Luna

[4.] http://www.menshealth.com/sex-women/sex-fetishes
Pakistanis Find Success In Fetish Business (2009)
Adam B. Ellick

[4.]
http://www.nytimes.com/2009/04/28/world/asia/28fetish.html? r=0
A Pakistani Underworld (2009)

Adam B. Ellick

[4.] http://www.nytimes.com/video/world/1194839708301/ a-pakistani-underworld.html?smid=tw-share

Adam B. Elick

# About the Author

PVC Leatherman worked in the retail and corporate world. It was while working in corporate, that he started his first foot fetish site, mainly out of frustration with the content he found on existing ones. He was also fed up with incommunicado producers who put their pockets ahead of their members and fans. His style of conducting interviews when combined with his creative photography and video work, took his sites to wildly popular levels with members, fans, and other producers in the foot fetish community. He mentored new producers and fans, and learned things from them as well.

Leatherman discovered an entirely new world, an underworld, when he did a foot fetish shoot with internationally-famous DJ and fetish model, Evilyn13. While there, the warm welcomes and encouragement he received from a group of people whom he didn't understand, but were intrigued by, led him to go to his first fetish party. There he met other like-minded individuals from all walks of life, which brings us here, to this very book in your hands. He hopes you enjoy reading it as much as he enjoys living it and writing about it!

# Table of Contents

# Shoulder Pain

## The Solution & Prevent
Shoulder Pain In Just 5

# Introduction

Shoulder pain is one of the more common issues that people often face. This is usually due to injuries that are not very serious in terms of being life threatening, but there are a few medical conditions that require you to get a checkup if you experience specific symptoms. The purpose of this guide is to help you relieve the pain found in your shoulder(s), and also to strengthen the shoulder region in order to possibly prevent the pain from happening again.

The information herein is offered for informational purposes solely, and is universal as so. The presentation of the information is without contract or any type of guarantee assurance.

The trademarks that are used are without any consent, and the publication of the trademark is without permission or backing by the trademark owner. All trademarks and brands within this book are for clarifying purposes only and are the owned by the owners themselves, not affiliated with this document.

# Understanding the Anatomy
# of Your Shoulders

You could be any age, gender, or ethnicity and still manage to experience shoulder pain at some point in your lifetime. The reason why generally has to do with the amount of use your shoulders go through on a daily basis. They are similar to your legs in that they are in almost just as much constant use as them, but the exception is that the shoulder joints are the most mobile group your body has.

These joints are capable of rotating the arm 360 degrees in a circular motion, and then they can move your shoulder back or forward, and you can also manipulate your shoulder to move up and away from your body. However, the term "shoulder" is a reference to multiple joints connected by tendons and muscle tissues. Your shoulders have the ability to enable multiple joint usages to accomplish a common goal, such as reaching that itch on your back, but this is sometimes a bad situation for your shoulders since that means more areas are capable of injury.

Nobody will really ever know when the shoulder pain is about to take place, but here is a list of reasons why it may occur, which preventive measures may be taken to keep the pain from being able to manifest in the first place.

- Lack of mobility and flexibility
- Weak shoulder joints
- Weak muscles surrounding joint
- Overuse
- Improper posture
- Mental stress

Shoulder pain usually derives from multiple reasons instead of just one. Uncovering the reason(s) behind your shoulder pain is the first step in relieving and preventing this type of injury. Let's take a look at the various reasons why you may be facing pain in this area of focus.

## Lack of Mobility and Flexibility

Mobility and flexibility greatly affect your range of motion (ROM) because these two factors allow proper movement to take place. Usually we hear the two terms being used interchangeably, but they are two different focuses that must be addressed as separate entities. Mobility is everything that revolves around the movement of a joint, which would be soft tissue, bone strength, ROM, and even motor control. Flexibility, on the other hand, focuses more on just the ligaments and soft tissues surrounding the shoulder joint.

Personal trainers and physical therapists focus on these two factors more than anything else, and they are generally the most common reason behind oncoming shoulder pain. The ability to place your shoulders in different positions comes from multiple areas working together with the shoulder region such as your chest, neck, and upper arms. Even people who actively participate in weight lifting face the possibility of shoulder pain from the lack of mobility and flexibility.

For example, a man who frequently lifts weight five days a week feels a lot of pain starting to take place. He performs exercises with proper form and never over trains his muscles, but for some reason the pain still happens. The reason why is because the exercises we see being performed in the gym such as bench pressing and biceps curls do little for the actual muscles and ligaments assisting with shoulder movement.

This is where functional training and active stretching actually help your shoulders through exercising instead doing more harm. This type of training will be covered in more details later in this guide.

# Weak Shoulder Joints

As mentioned, your shoulder joints can become injured easily if you are not attempting to make them stronger. A mixture of strength and functional training with particular interests in nutrition are the best way to solve this issue. Strength training focuses on making your muscles, joints, ligaments, and bones capable of withstanding pressure from external forces. This type of training is not going to make your body look like a bodybuilder, so it is completely fine for both men and women to participate in

# Weak Muscles Surrounding Joint

This is not referencing the actual muscles around the shoulder joint itself, but the ones that enable the movement of your shoulders. Typical exercises are going to enhance the muscles that people want others to notice such as the chest, back, and arms muscles, but often time's people forget about the smaller muscle groups causing muscle imbalances, which is when muscle groups become larger than others. This causes us to lose flexibility and our range of motion suffers. The extra effort that your shoulders have to perform to overcome tight muscles leads to the shoulder pain.

# Shoulder Overuse

You do not have to be exercising for shoulder pain to arise from overuse. Daily activities from work and even being at home can become the problem in this situation. Overuse of your shoulders is implying something that is routinely happening placing them under more stress than the average person. For example, if you keep items at the very top of a cabinet and constantly pull them down, the shoulder is being overused throughout the years, which slowly causes pain.

Work related shoulder overuse is very common as well amongst those who move supplies and equipment throughout the day. Constant movement to pick up an item, carrying it, and placing the item where it goes causes multiple forms of stress on your shoulder. Long durations of overuse are possibly going to cause osteoarthritis, which is commonly referred to as the wear-and-tear of all types of arthritis. This type of arthritis is slow to form and become even noticeable, which is why taking preventive measures earlier keeps it away longer.

# Improper Posture

This is another common reason for shoulder pain during these technological times. Everything from working on the computer to sitting on the couch watching television causes shoulders to fall forward, which is why so many people these days are hunched over. This forward-leaning type of posture is referred to as being kyphotic. If your posture is bad enough the shoulders will begin to ache at first, and then progress into recurring sharp pain over time.

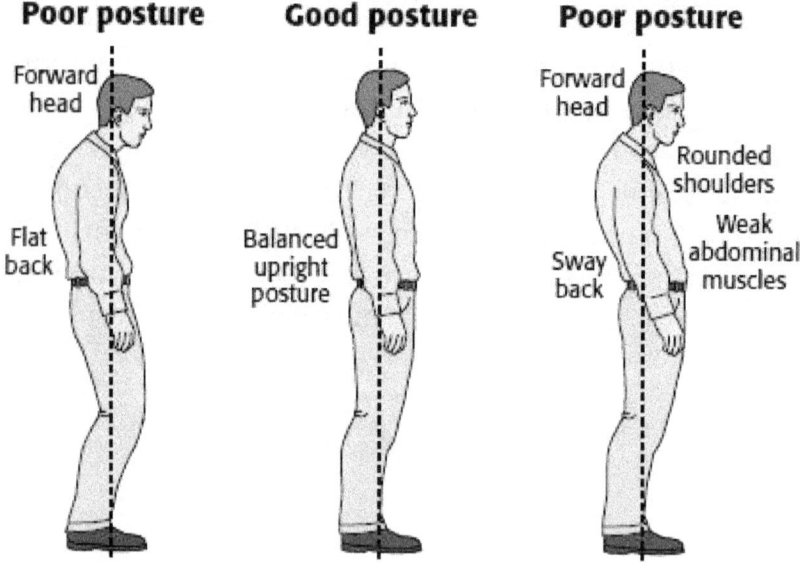

A video demonstrating what good posture looks like:
https://youtu.be/J6E-moCgG1E

# Mental Stress

Stress might sound a bit odd for being the root problem of shoulder pain, but research has proven that it causes a lot of issues within our bodies, so the theory is not too farfetched. The reason why mental stress would affect your shoulders is because biochemical and neuromuscular stress based responses may cause improper signals to be sent to the shoulder region, causing harm and pain.

One or more of these factors could be the cause of your shoulder pain injury taking place, but are not the actual initiators that cause the pain to take place. Usually performing a simple task such as reaching behind the driver's seat in the car will cause a strain that makes the pain come about. Exercises and stretches are capable of keeping this from happening by strengthening your body and loosening up tight muscle fibers.

# Exercises that Prevent Shoulder Pain

Exercising and stretching on a routine basis is one of the best ways to prevent shoulder pains. There really is no need to lift heavy weights when trying to strengthen your shoulder muscles and joints, and instead you should stick with lifting moderate weights if your body is healthy; and then light to no weights if you are recovering from a painful shoulder injury and/or surgery. The best way to accomplish strengthening your entire body together is through compound lifting and functional training.

## Compound Lifts

These lifts target multiple joints and muscle groups opposed to isolation lifts, which target a specific muscle group. People often assume that isolating their shoulders will help prevent any injuries from occurring, but this could actually have a negative effect instead of positive outcome. The reason for this is because over time the focused training causes the shoulders to wear down even faster, thus possibly increasing the chances of osteoporosis.

On the other hand, compound lifts are placing the external force against multiple joints to help distribute the impact, which allows all or most muscle groups to contract and benefit from this type of training. Primary compound lifts include chest press, military press, squats, lunges, pull-ups, and deadlifts. All of these exercises help strengthen your muscles to prevent joint pain, and your shoulders will welcome the fact that not all the work is being placed upon them.

However, there is another type of training that surpasses compound lifts because they focus more on the muscles that involve daily functions such as reaching, lifting, walking up stairs, etc. This is referred to as functional training, which is used for keeping your joints, muscles, and bones in healthy condition to prevent injuries such as shoulder pains from occurring.

## Functional Training

Being functionally fit means that you can properly perform daily tasks outside of the gym, during work, and while on your own free time. Basically this means it is being able to simply move and live. Functional training is similar to compound training since it involves multiple muscle groups and joints, but it differs because it also includes unconventional methods as well. Conventional methods are those that are in a stable environment with balanced resistance such as dumbbells, barbells, and weight machines.

Unconventional means that the equipment being used is not properly balanced and the environment is not always stable, which is much like how life functions. The equipment used for this would be ropes, sledge hammers, tires, sandbags, and most importantly – kettlebells. Kettlebells are known for being the best functional training based equipment that is available and capable of increasing strength throughout the body.

There is no other equipment available that allows you to place your shoulders, and muscles that support the shoulders, in the same range of motion as the kettlebell. All you would need is one of these that weight enough to provide resistance, but light enough to perform all exercises and keep from injuring your body. You must be able to properly perform the exercises prior to increasing any weight amounts or repetitions, and the reason for this is because most pain injuries received from training are developed from improperly performing exercises.

The following exercises combine both categories of training into a physical training program designed to keep your shoulders strong and durable against any pains that can occur:

|  | Sets | Reps |
|---|---|---|
| • Kettlebell Swings – | x3 | x10 |
| • Turkish Get Ups – Arms Each Set) | x3 | x5 (Alternate |
| • Windmills – Arms Each Set) | x2 | x8 (Alternate |
| • Clean and Press - | x3 | x10 |
| • Dips – | x3 | x12 |
| • Overhead Press to Lunges – | x3 | x10 |
| • Halo's – | x2 | x8 |
| • Hanging Straight Leg Lifts - | x1 | Failure Set |

## Kettlebell How To's

Kettlebell Swings: https://youtu.be/q0jalJ-3e7U

KB Turkish Get Ups: https://youtu.be/uGRBvom4Zrw

KB Windmills: https://youtu.be/6651sjanpxI

KB Clean and Press: https://youtu.be/kpy25FN_w4w

KB Dips: https://youtu.be/gIyVqxLhMsc

KB Overhead Press to Lunge:
https://youtu.be/eClosHxzY9E

KB Halos: https://youtu.be/Ia7_h43xjpY

KB Hanging Straight Leg Raises:
https://youtu.be/x8Nd8OchL5o

## Exercises For Shoulder Pain (Without a Kettlebell)

Excercises for Shoulder pain video:
https://youtu.be/c0_qtY5kX_g

# What to do if Shoulder Pain Persists

If the shoulder pain comes back again then you have to think about several factors:

- Form used during training

- Weight used for resistance

- Tight muscles that need a warm-up

As mentioned previously, proper form plays a major role in the outcome of your exercise program. You can easily injure your shoulders if you perform exercises such as the barbell chest press, but this could also mean that the exercise is not ready for you just yet. For example, use dumbbells instead of a barbell for the chest press. People often find that they are just not getting used to this type of simultaneous movement, so the dumbbells offset the restrictions of a barbell. This will then allow you to see if one side of your body is progressing faster than the other i.e. you can lift more weight in one arm compared to the other.

Lowering the amount of weight you chose for training would be your next step. This plays into form as well since you are not going to be able to perform an exercise properly if you do not have the strength required. Then you have muscles that are being sent into contraction while they are still tight and tense. Various studies show that warming up prior to training prevents a large percentage of possible training injuries. A proper warm-up is performed with various stretching techniques, which we will cover more in-depth in the next chapter.

# Stretches that Prevent Shoulder Pain

A warm-up is basically performing various stretching techniques for a minimum of five minutes, which prepares your body's muscles for contractions of longer durations. Frequently performing stretching exercises and yoga training allows the flexibility of your joints to increase as well. The overall benefits of performing a warm-up with stretches prior to training or performing general daily tasks are:

- Proven increases to flexibility

- Risk of injury is minimized due to joints being placed into their full range of motion without strain on ligaments.

- Everyday tasks can be accomplished more efficiently with little injury of risk from performing daily skills such as lifting a box.

- Blood circulation is increased from flexibility, which is increased from stretching. This allows blood to carry oxygen and nutrients to muscle much quicker.

- Tight muscles cause the body to have bad posture. Stretching allows good posture by loosening the muscles gradually.

- Muscle tension is relieved through relaxed muscles after stretching has occurred.

All of this combined allows you to prevent shoulder pain or injuries, but there are several types of stretching that need to be given priority since they will benefit you greater than others. The stretching techniques you want to focus on for shoulder pain prevention are:

- Static Stretching

- Passive Stretching

- Dynamic Stretching

The three stretching techniques are all you really need to focus on. They are pretty simple and straightforward with what purpose they serve, and can be combined together during the warm-up phase prior to training, which is actually recommended instead of just choosing one or the other.

# Static Stretching

Static stretches are the most commonly used stretch for all different purposes ranging from sports to office work. There is no proven benefit that they assist with sports performance, but they are proven to increase flexibility and range of motion more significantly than those that do not perform them. A static stretch means you take and hold the stretch for a specific time frame. Being more specific, the muscle group and joints are going to be stretched to their maximum points, which you will then hold this stretch for a minimum of 30 seconds to actually benefit from the. This is the safest stretch available to use with little worry of injury.

An example of a static stretch would be taking one arm and stretching across your chest to the opposite shoulder. Then you would hold the stretch for the designated time frame and alternate arms.

1 minute shoulder stretch routine:
https://youtu.be/wnlcuZomJSU

Shoulder Stretch Video: https://youtu.be/4wYLZdgvUfY

# Passive Stretching

Static stretching is known as an active stretch, which is when you create the intensity of the resistance. However, there is another form of static stretching that is referred to as being passive, which means you are not the one cause the intensity of the resistance, and instead an external force from a device or partner is going to be doing this for you. They are pretty similar in the benefits being sought, but passive stretches allow a better stretching intensity to take place that a normal person cannot accomplish on their own.

An example of a passive stretch would be if you lied on your back, and then a partner pushes your foot towards your body to stretch the hamstrings.

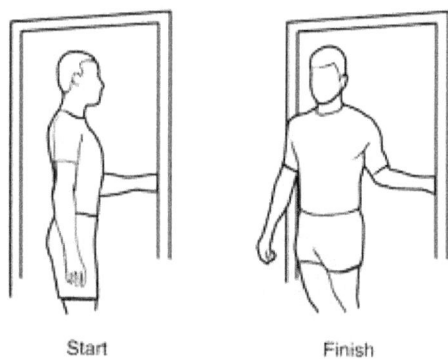

Start          Finish

Passive stretching video: https://youtu.be/fr6pCpNEAz4

Two stretches to cure bad shoulders:
https://youtu.be/c2uVtX44nfg

# Dynamic Stretching

This type of stretching is actually proven to help increase sports performance, which means it is functionally capable of strengthening your joints and allowing tight muscle fibers the chance to warm-up as well. Dynamic stretching differs from the other two because you are actively placing your muscles and joints into various movements. Athletes would perform dynamic stretches that pertain to their particular sport, and the average person performs exercises that assist with moving the body around during the day.

An example of a dynamic stretch would be arm circles, which allows the shoulders to move 360 degrees to increase ROM, flexibility, and possibly prevent shoulder pain.

Dynamic stretching video: https://youtu.be/Z4c95kosHes

**Shoulder Stretches to Consider:**

- Arm-Across Chest Stretch
  Video: https://youtu.be/yJiixnuBTqc
- Shoulder Blade Squeezes
  Video: https://youtu.be/9tJTdqUXW14
- Alternating Side Neck Stretch
  Video: https://youtu.be/oFuYstVevAc
- Shoulder Flexion
  Video: https://youtu.be/f-Xiq00YDOI
- Shoulder Abduction
  Video: https://youtu.be/qRlQcthZoQk
- Shoulder Rolls
  Video: https://youtu.be/cJXquDX3DcM
- Wide Arm Circles
  Video: https://youtu.be/6KPD7Mr7Yjk

# Yoga Training for
# Shoulder Pain Prevention

The three stretching techniques discussed are the easiest form of stretching you can perform on a daily basis, which work a lot better if performed prior to any training or heavy lifting. However, you can take a step further by performing yoga once or twice a week to strengthen your shoulders and other important joints across your body. You do not need an actual class to benefit from beginner yoga stretches since there are a lot of references to refer to across the Internet. Joint strengthening, flexibility, ROM, increased blood circulation, and increased mobility are just a few of the benefits received from yoga, and even professional athletes perform yoga regularly these days.

All the exercises and stretches presented to you can be performed by anybody from the beginning stages of training to the advanced athletes. However, you should take it easy if you are first starting out, and only perform two sets for all the exercises and stretches provided. This ensures that your muscles and joints are not going to be at risk of injury.

# Treating and Recovering
# from Shoulder Pain

We are recommended to prevent injuries before they arise, but this is not usually the case for most. The average person is going to experience shoulder pain before they start to take preventive steps towards it in the future, so the question is what should you do once the pain occurs? The following is general information that has been compiled to help treat the shoulder pain and allow recovery, but should not be used in place of your primary physician's advice. Let's take a look at treating minor shoulder pain first.

Minor shoulder pain means that you feel throbbing in your shoulder and may have lost some mobility due to the injury. Serious shoulder pain injuries last longer than a week and could possibly cause loss of all shoulder mobility, and/or cause excruciating pain. Serious shoulder pains need to be seen by a doctor immediately, but there are methods we can use to alleviate minor shoulder pains.

# Temperature Therapy

The most common route people choose to take is using some form of a pain relieving medicine to help reduce the pain, but sometimes this is not going to help very much on its own, and swelling needs a little more than just medication. Temperature therapy includes heat and ice therapy, which have their unique benefits for assisting with shoulder pain. **Ice therapy** is used to reduce swelling in the area of pain and numb the area to reduce the feelings caused by the injury. This is usually applied with cold therapy gel packs, a bag of ice, or even frozen vegetable packs of loose veggies such as corn. Ice therapy is for short term use only and generally applied the day of the injury.

**Heat therapy** is used to relax muscles and soothe stiff joints. You would usually perform this after the swelling has subsided and pain has been reduced. This type of therapy allows you to proceed on with the recovery process, and is capable of being used for longer periods than ice therapy. Low-level heat therapy is capable of being used for up to eight hours, and is intended for those who feel the pain is being alleviated by heat therapy. The equipment used for this can be found in most drug stores, and you have to read the instructions carefully since it is for longer durations.

Regardless of the temperature therapy you choose to use for shoulder pain, you are advised to use a pillowcase or something similar to go between your skin and the treatment pack. This protects your outer skin from the extreme temperatures it is not used to having placed upon it.

# Exercises and Stretches for Recovery

Some of the ones you use for recovery are similar to preventive exercises and stretches, but there are other variations you should consider when you are on the road to recovery from shoulder pain. Only perform these once you feel it is safe for your shoulders to begin recovery, or if your physician has given you the clear to take action. Although it may sound odd, but joints and muscles recover better and faster through active movement opposed to being sedentary, which is slower and may hinder the recovery process without some type of activity. This is why people are not recommended to be on bed rest for too long.

Prior to performing any of the following exercises or stretches for recovery, you are recommended to warm-up by walking at a higher pace for 8-10 minutes. Each exercise should be performed no more than 3 sets for 10 reps. Stretches should be lightly intensified and last no longer than 20 seconds. Remember, you are recovering and taking it easy, so nothing too intense should be taking place.

- **Pendular Exercises** – This exercise allows your shoulders to be placed into abduction and flexion positions. You perform them by leaning forward and bracing one arm on something sturdy that keeps you propped up. Allow the arm with the shoulder pain to dangle loosely, and proceed to move it forward, backwards, and then left to right.
  Video of technique: https://youtu.be/9-DOa672Hxk

- **Pendular Circles** – You get into position with this exercise the same way as the previous one, but instead you rotate the arm with shoulder pain in a circle forward and reverse.
  Video of technique: https://youtu.be/VRodFwbuF-g

- **Fingertip Wall Crawl** – Wall crawls allow you to slowly get used to raising your arm above your head again. You place your fingertips on the wall with the arm experiencing shoulder pain at shoulder height. Slowly "walk" your fingertips up the wall.
  Video of technique: https://youtu.be/CpDEEAfyNSA

- **External Shoulder Rotation** – Stand with your body fully erect and place the lower arm of the shoulder in pain to be parallel with the floor, and elbow tucked naturally against your side. Proceed to rotate your lower arm towards your back as if opening a door.

- **Passive External Rotation** – This is the same movement as the previous exercise, but has assistance from a straight stick such as a broom handle. People use this exercise if they require assistance for the external rotation.

You can combine these previous stretches and exercises discussed already if your shoulder in pain is capable of performing more intense ranges of motion:

- Arm-Across Chest Stretch

- Shoulder Flexion

- Shoulder Abduction

Temperature therapy and intentional recovery movements are the best methods available that increase the recovery time and ease the pain away. Results are not always seen or noticed quickly, so give it a few days of attempting before feeling like something else needs to be done. This will save you a lot of money and time if the shoulder pain injury is minor and not in need of medical assistance.

# The Bottom Line for Shoulder Pain

Shoulder pain is capable of being prevented and treated if it should arise. However, prevention does not come naturally especially as you begin to age, so it takes initiative to start taking the steps necessary to keeping the injuries away. Your shoulders are quite strong and durable, and the usual reason pain tends to come to them is because of the muscles surrounding the joint, and not the joint itself.

We discussed that a primary method for preventing injuries to your shoulder joints would be strengthening and stretching the muscles surrounding your shoulders. A lot of muscles connect to this region, and the safest thing to consider would be to train each muscle group once a week to prevent excessive training of one area, which could lead to shoulder pain.

Specialized training revolves around training a target area for 3-4 days a week, and is not recommended for those who are not advanced in physical training. The only exception would be focusing on your shoulders during the recovery process, which does not use and weighted resistance and can be performed as many days in a row you want. The reason for this is because it is maintenance and recovery training – muscle building is not really a focus at this stage of recovery.

During days of regular strength training it is advised that you take at least 24-48 hours of rest to allow complete recovery of the skeletal muscles used during that training day. Rest does not just mean the time spent away from training, but refers to the time you are actually sleeping as well. Your body needs rest from proper sleeping cycles to allow your shoulders the chance to recover and receive valuable nutrients for this process. Protein is the primary nutrient responsible for muscle and bone repair, but carbs and dietary fats should be consumed daily in moderate amounts as well.

Attempt to prevent shoulder pain before it starts with all the information provided to you in this article. However, it is not 100% guaranteed to prevent injuries, but rather used to decrease the chances significantly. In conclusion, you need to stretch and exercise your shoulders while consuming the proper nutrients and getting plenty of sleep if you wish to possibly keep shoulder pain away.

www.ingramcontent.com/pod-product-compliance
Lightning Source LLC
Chambersburg PA
CBHW070247290526
45789CB00004B/1802